MY RESUME IS GREAT

I think ™

...SO WHY DIDN'T I GET AN INTERVIEW?

Fast and easy guide for
people with 5+ years of professional
work experience to write a resume
that *gets interviews!*

STACIE GARLIEB

TABLE OF CONTENTS

Introduction   **v**

*My choice of resume format
best represents my skills* I think ...   **1**

My 'Contact Information' is complete I think ...   **3**

*My 'Objective' or 'Professional Summary'
is clear* I think ...   **7**

My 'Education' information is crystal clear I think ...   **9**

*My 'Work Experience' makes me
a good candidate* I think ...   **13**

My 'Military Experience' section is thorough I think ...   **19**

*My 'Organization and/or Volunteer Experience'
section shows everything I did* I think ...   **21**

*My 'Professional Affiliations' show my
industry interest* I think ...   **25**

My 'Licenses and Certifications' are relevant I think ...   **27**

*My 'Technical/Computer Skills'
section explains my abilities* I think ...   **29**

*My 'Language Skills' section
accurately represents me* I think ...   **31**

My resume is ready to go I think ...
— Checklist before you send your resume out!   **33**

'Before' and 'After' Resume Examples   **36**

Index   **55**

My resume is great I think
...so why didn't I get an interview?©

INTRODUCTION

You had a friend review your resume, you compared it to a colleague's, you used it to interview for your last job and got hired, so why isn't your resume getting the attention of recruiters and hiring managers for interviews now?

There could be one or more reasons, so this book is intended to help you find ways to make your resume more impactful and user-friendly to a recruiter and hiring manager.

The 'we' in the book is referring to a combined collaboration of recruiters, HR managers, and hiring managers who are currently in positions reviewing resumes everyday. 'We' know what good looks like, and what bad looks like. Resume review is either the best or worst part of the day for managers, so this book is written to make reading your resume a positive experience which stands out from the other candidates!

Take the sections one by one and evaluate what you are starting with. Be honest about what works and doesn't work for the field you are entering, (we give you some ways to figure out what may and may not work). Don't get emotionally attached to your resume – it's a business document that should be living and breathing and being updated monthly throughout your career. Overall, your resume needs to be the initial introduction to an employer that tells them what you can bring to their team.

• • •

My choice of resume format best represents my skills **I think** ...

There are two basic types of resumes that can be used to represent your skills to a prospective hiring manager either internally in your current company, or for a job in another company. Choosing which format will work for your skills and industry experience is an important first step.

Most familiar to all of us is the 'chronological format'. This resume will start with your most recent work experience first, then next recent, then next recent, and so on. Recruiters and hiring managers see this format most of the time, so it makes it easy to see 'what are you doing now' to 'what have you done in the past'. The downsides of a chronological resume could include the following:

- I have a 'gap' in my employment...
    - A chronological resume will 'show' this gap in bright lights. Under our current economy, this is not as big of a deal as it would have been in the job market in 2005 though. Hiring personnel know that people may be in transition from jobs for reasons beyond their control.

- I am applying for a position that needs skills that I did in a job years ago but not recently...
    - The challenge for a chronological resume in this scenario is that the person reading it may discount you as a candidate before they can 'scan' down to the position where you

used these skills. Functional formatted resumes would probably be best in this situation.

So the alternative is to create a 'functional format' resume. Functional resumes use headings/categories of skills to highlight information that would most relevant to the employer, industry, or position you are applying for. Headings would be titled based on your skill set – Managerial Experience, Project Management Experience, Sales and Marketing Experience – and then have reverse chronological information of the jobs where you got that experience under each section.

The functional format definitely has more room for error. The biggest challenge is making sure information is not duplicated under sections and keeping the responsibilities/headings, in addition to the content for bullet points under each job listing, clear for a recruiter or hiring manager. You can refer to the functional formatted resume example in the back of the book to see if this format would work for your current situation. Writing a chronological resume first and THEN making the content fit a functional format would be easiest in most cases.

Remember the part about updating your resume every month? That means you may have a chronological format that you keep as your 'master' for updating, and then a functional format would be a 'backup' for certain career opportunities as they come up. As you move through your career, you could use both formats at different times. It is also a good idea to save your resume as First name Last name Resume Month Year (Tom Smith) for your file name. That will let hiring managers know that they have the most current version of your resume.

. . .

My 'Contact Information' is complete I think ...

The first piece of information at the top of your resume is your name. It isn't necessary to be overly formal with what name you use, and in fact we would rather see what name you go by in the workplace. If your legal name is James and everyone calls you Jim, then it is appropriate to put 'Jim' on your resume. Unless your middle name goes along with your first name (people call you Mary Jo and your name is Mary Joanne), or it has cultural relevance that you would like an employer to know about, you can leave that off. When you fill out an application we will find that out.

Next is your address, which should always be included. A home address would be the first choice, but a PO box is fine. Contacting a company with a job in a city you want to relocate to? Then put an address of someone you know, if you can, who lives in that specific city you are interested in relocating to. Just be aware that you will need to explain that you are planning to relocate and are not in that location yet.

A phone number is next (yes, ONE phone number, not 2 or 3 numbers....). Number one choice in this case is your cell number, that way you can control the messages and when you retrieve them. And once you start the job search process, don't answer unless you recognize the number! We could be calling you for a spontaneous phone interview and talking while you are grocery shopping or driving somewhere would not be the place for you to be when representing your skills.

Let's say you are posting for an internal position at your current employer. Then your extension at the company would be the best number, because it shows the hiring manager that you already work there. The advantage of contacting you for a phone interview is that you already know the company, the culture, and they can also talk with your current manager to see if you are a 'fit' for the other position.

By the way, we don't need your fax number. If we need to fax you, we will let you know and you can give us the number then. That is a 'space filler upper' – information that isn't relevant and just takes up space on the page.

Last, but VERY important is the email address. Some people have really creative email addresses, BUT a resume is not the time to have 'susanlovesdogs@aol.com' shared with the working world. First name (first initial).last name @ whatever search engine you want to use is the best format. Check your spam file regularly when you are applying for positions because some search engines will default extensions there.

Some industries may want to see your abilities by requesting relevant documents from your work (a portfolio if you are an artist or photographer, press releases or writing samples for journalism or public relations etc.). If you choose to use LinkedIn® or a blog or personal website to include this content, you can note that URL on your resume under your email address too.

What about applying internally? Same situation as on the phone number – put your internal email address. In both of these cases, you need to be ok with the hiring manager contacting your current boss. That may be the first phone call he makes to see what your current performance level is. If you are looking to make a transition without your current manager's support or knowledge, then put your personal cell phone and personal (professional format) email address.

Here's an example (and there are more in the back – check out the 'Before and After' Resumes)

Bob Smith

123 N. First Street

Anytown, Anywhere 00000

(555) 555-1212

Firstname.lastname@searchengine.com

www.urlforportfolio.searchengine

• • •

My 'Objective' or 'Professional Summary' is clear I think ...

We know that your Objective is 'to get a job' or 'further my career opportunities' – what we really want to know is, "what's in it for ME" the employer to invite you to interview? What skills are the employer looking for that you have? What position are you applying for specifically? An Objective will put that information into one brief sentence.

Here's an example:

Objective: To maximize productivity and revenue as a Territory Sales Representative with XYZ Company by using my communication, organization, and customer service skills.

The key is to keep an Objective short and direct. Employers know why you are sending them a resume but this tells them a few reasons to keep reading and find out more about the skills you listed; where did you get them and what impact did you make with them?

Another way to show what skills make you 'stand out' as a candidate is to put a Professional Summary. Don't put both on your resume. In most cases, a Professional Summary will be for candidates who have been in more than one position and have mastered certain skills that the employer is looking for. Someone with five years of administrative experience may put an Objective, where someone with ten years of people and project management experience would possibly be better served with a Professional Summary.

A Professional Summary should still be brief, but you may include information about the extent of experience you have in a specific area for that industry. This way we know what skills you are going to 'bring to the table' and then we can look for those in the bullet points under your work experience.

Here's an example:

Professional Summary: Corporate manager with over ten years of experience in sports marketing, sales, product branding, client partnership, and business development, with skills to enable an organization to exceed marketing and business growth goals.

Be careful of the content in the Professional Summary though – it should be a 'teaser' to make the recruiter want to read your WHOLE resume. If it looks like you are just condensing content that should be in the body of your resume, some recruiters will not read any further. The goal is still to be brief and it should be a summary– not a novel!

When you aren't sure which way to go, an Objective is always easier to write and accepted as standard by recruiters and hiring managers.

• • •

My 'Education' information is

crystal clear I think ...

Where you are going and or went to school could take primary position after the Objective or Professional Summary, depending on how long ago you graduated or if you have returned to get a higher degree and are in the process of finishing it currently. General rule of thumb is if you have graduated more than a year ago and have been in the 'working world' since then, your education could go in either first or second to last position. If you graduated more than two years ago, move this section down to right above your 'Technical' and 'Computer' skills sections.

There are a million different descriptions of majors and minors (and we've seen them all), so it's important to let us know what type you got or are going to complete, a Bachelor of Science, Bachelor of Arts, Associates, or Masters of whatever degree. Minors and Certificates get listed next along with the specialty they are covering.

Instead of listing the 'year in school' you are in (if applicable), just let us know the month and year you are going to graduate – it's not necessary to add "Expected to graduate", "Will Graduate" etc – employers do know that if it is 2018 and you put 2022 you have not completed your degree yet.

Dean's List, or any academic awards, should get their own line if possible! Academic performance is one way to separate yourself from the competition. Did you get a scholarship for GPA and other criteria – put it here. National honors organizations (ones where you get the piece of paper but there isn't any meeting to go to such as Golden Key) can be listed here too.

High school information should only be included if it is the highest level of education you have completed. If you are entering your junior year of a collegiate program, high school information should not be included unless it is relevant to the specific employer's interests (i.e.: if the hiring manager went there too). At that point, employers are focusing on how you have spent the past two years of school (or more if you have an Associates degree too).

So the debate over whether to show your GPA continues....this is a personal decision but we would like to see anything over a 3.0 (or 'B' average) on the resume. Let's say you received your degree more than 2 years ago then you could leave your GPA off – but if you graduated with honors based on it, include it. Showing academic performance tells an employer that you know how to learn – that's a valuable skill. If you do include it, please round your GPA to one decimal point – it's not like 'Pi' (aka: 3.14159....)!

Education:	**New State University**	New Town, State	May 2017
	Really Important Person School of Business		
	Bachelor of Science in Business		
	Minor: Business Communication		GPA: 3.2
	Dean's List Spring 2014, Fall 2015		
	Golden Key National Honor Society Member		

Should you include 'Relevant Courses'? Depends on whether the course is unique to your area of specialization (i.e.: Consumer Behavior in US Retailers) that the company – say a large retailer – would be interested in the content. Did you do a semester long project that would be relevant? That could be a bullet point under the course title:

Special Course:

Consumer Behavior in US Retailers   September 2017

♦ Recognized by project review panel of mass merchandiser retail executives with highest class grade.

• • •

Here's what NOT to do – don't list the core curriculum you have taken. We actually know that a marketing major has to take marketing classes to graduate. Only focus on classes that may be interesting and special to the company receiving the resume and be ready to talk about large projects from the class in an interview.

If you studied overseas, here is a great place to make your resume stand out! Traveling with your friends for a few days doesn't count. Make sure you include the name of the university program, dates, location you lived, and what you studied. Showing you can speak a foreign language can be highlighted here (and repeated in a separate section of your resume) too.

Not everyone is going to have all of this – that is what makes each resume individualized.

International School Overseas   Overseas, Country   Summer 2018
- Qualified for two month program based on GPA, essay, and interview process.
- Learned how to fluently speak Alpha by interacting and living with a Country family.
- Completed courses in culture, language, art, and business in Country.

• • •

My 'Work Experience' makes me a good candidate I think ....

The key to an impactful work experience section is having information we want to know – what company did you work for, where did you do the work (city, state), when did you do the work, what was your title, what responsibilities/activities/projects did you have and what results did you achieve. Internships and externships– even if you didn't get paid – are work, and employers find great candidates with real-world experience and skills from those positions being included on resumes.

Most important part of each job's information is the 'what responsibilities/activities/projects did you have and what results did you achieve'. Unfortunately, this is also the section most likely to sound like a 'Miss America' answer. Please don't write a paragraph – hiring managers see hundreds of resumes for some positions, so bullet points are easier to read. Next, a bullet point shouldn't be able to be finished with 'create world peace' or 'solve world hunger' (the Miss America part). If it is too fluffy or lacking the results you achieved with the skills or responsibility, think about changing the content to make it more real.

A magic formula to make the bullet points 'real' is to add numerical or specific data for the results part. Strong bullet points will have at least 3 of these five criteria:

S pecific
M easurable (how many/much)
A ction-oriented (action verbs)
R esults (numbers or goals met)
T ime bound (over what time period)

Part of this formula is easy because it just takes changing 'soft' verbs to 'action verbs' at the beginning of the bullet point. :

- ◆ Responsible for cash and credit transactions and tracking

Changes to:

- ◆ Balanced cash and credit receipts to 100% for register transactions totaling up to $5,000 per day.

Notice that change also added in the 'M', and 'R', and 'T'.... Not every bullet point will hit three criteria without some tweaking. The more specific and results oriented your bullets are, the better we can evaluate whether you have the skills we are looking for.
Part of making every resume different to meet the needs of what the employer is looking for is to move the bullet points around in order. If I am looking for a Management Candidate, then someone who has 'Collaborated', 'Directed', 'Coordinated', 'Managed', as bullet points in first position under the applicable job is probably going to get a first interview to see if they can really explain their skills in that area.

The next question is 'Which work experience should I include?' – the easy answer is anything you developed or used real-world skills in. If you have worked in a restaurant or retail store, you may have had a difficult customer or a challenging situation with someone ordering/ buying something they didn't like. Those situations use problem-solving skills, and you probably used your communication skills to resolve it. No matter what industry or company you are pursuing an opportunity in, those are valuable skills.

Office work, or work with children or 'on campus' work, all use organization, communication, and time management skills. Think about what you did and what you learned from it. Let's say you didn't learn anything new, but you mastered a skill (computer programs, organization of an office, using a database or phone system) – that's valuable because then an employer knows that you are willing to learn in the workplace!

• • •

This doesn't mean to over-elaborate on your experience. Be careful of the 'Miss America' factor – if we think you "made up" one thing, we may think other parts are made up too. Make sure you are truthful and accurate so when you get to the interview you can use those bullet points to develop stories about what skills you bring to the table.

Here are some of examples of work experience sections:

ABC Coffee Company   Town, State   Summers 2015, 2016
Coffee Maker

- ♦ Collaborated with team of 4 employees for 8 hour shift achieving store revenue goal of $3K daily.
- ♦ Exceeded daily sales goals by 55% per management direction with over 250 customer interactions.
- ♦ Managed opening and closing store including all daily finance and inventory activities at highest volume New State store.
- ♦ Learned how to effectively use visual merchandising to maximize revenue in 3 window and 5 in-store displays.

Non-Profit Company People Town, Old State September 2017 – Present
Marketing Assistant

- ♦ Assist in creation of nine promotional pieces for fundraising events resulting in 1000 people attending.
- ♦ Research fifty marketing contacts for support and contact them weekly via email and phone.
- ♦ Coordinated silent auction items for display with 100% purchase at event end.
- ♦ Maximized donations from businesses through a database and follow up increasing future support.

John's Computer Company All Towns, New State July 2018 – Present
Sales Manager

- Direct operations and sales for a team of 15 representatives in six states to generate $25million in annual sales.
- Develop national client relationships including Big Tech Store Chain resulting in 105% performance 2009 versus 2008 sales goals.
- Created regional strategy to effectively promote more than 1500 products with 41% increase in seasonal sales.
- Assisted two managers with recruiting and hiring at three college campuses to create new districts in New State.

And you don't need to have 'four' bullet points per job either – these are just examples. A job that only has two bullet points could look weak though, so think about what you accomplished or learned and be specific about it. Make sure your bullet points make sense, so if you did it in the past, please use past tense, and if you are doing it still in that job, make it present tense. Whether you are an expert at the computer or not, please use 'Tools – Spelling and Grammar' before you send out a resume. Misspelled words will move your resume into the hiring manager's 'trash' very fast!

. . .

My 'Military Experience'

section is thorough I think ...

Military experience is highly valued by employers because of the structure, leadership, and training the military forces provide. The most important things to remember about highlighting this experience on your resume include the following:

- Years of service
  - If you are currently serving in the reserves, it is appropriate to put that as a separate bullet point under your active duty experience.

- Specific training
  - Training in specialized areas may or may not be relevant for potential opportunities. Since your resume should be tailored to each employer, the training you list in this section could change based on the position you are posting for.

- Discharge status
  - Honorable discharge could be listed with its own bullet point or as a part of the title you ended your service in.

- Special Assignments
  - Significant assignments which gave you skills that are relevant to the position you are applying for should definitely be included as a separate bullet point.

Just as in the 'Work Experience' section, the name of the armed forces branch, dates of service in various positions, general location or exact place stationed, and responsibilities and achievements should all be included.

United States Navy   International and US   August 2011 – August 2018
Information Technician 1st Class Petty Officer (Honorable Discharge)

- Managed team of 5 workers to provide support and mainte-nance of shipboard IT equipment.
- Developed and executed Security program with a training plan and documentation on consequences of violation for the crew.
- Created monthly plan for distribution of XYZ security patches, software upgrades, and system configuration changes resulting in reduced downtime for daily operations.
- Designated as Master Recruiter from July 2013 – November 2014.
- Earned "Admiral's Five Star Award" in May 2016 for meeting recruiting goals and ranked in the Top 10 regionally from over 45 recruiters.

. . .

My 'Organization and/or Volunteer Experience' section shows everything I did I think ....

In this section you want to include any organizations you have been actively involved in that provided you skills that are relevant to the job you are applying to including school organizations (i.e.: sorority that you are active in the alumnae association) if you are still involved.

Organizations that are specific to your personal life (PTA or Little League) could be relevant if you are holding a position that requires skills, like time management and communication, that an employer would be interested in. Be careful not to list personal organizations if they do not 'add' value to your other information on your resume. If you are already showing your time management and communication skills in 'work experience', then reiterating it in the organization section may not be applicable.

What if the organization is for recreation and you are passionate about the mission or activities of the group (Masonic Lodge, Book Club, Golf Team Club etc)? Then you could decide when to include that based on the job – if you find out the person you are sending the resume to lists golf as an interest on their Facebook® or LinkedIn® profile – you may want to put it in. If you don't know the person and can't make the call, leave it off unless you have/had a leadership position that shows skills you learned or mastered from being involved.

Not everyone is on 'council, executive board, committee chair' and that is fine. If you are/have been, make sure you include bullet points with your responsibilities – how many people 'reported' to you, did you manage a budget, were there reports that you submitted to the regional or national organization, what improvements or developments in the organization (recruitment of members, changing events, increasing local presence) did you work on and execute.

The bullet points need to be SMART – go back to the 'Work Experience' section for a quick reminder on this – and meaningful/ not obvious. If you are President of an organization, hiring managers know that you 'Led a chapter for annual events'. Create those bullet points to show the employer the specifics of what we won't automatically know about your organization.

If you are or were an active member, then include a bullet point (or more if applicable) about what programs/projects/events you participated to support the organization. Did you help with referrals of new members, what about philanthropies/charity events, was there a regional or national conference that you participated in representing the organization? And while you are updating your resume with this information, go to your LinkedIn® profile to add members of the organizations to your Connections – they could have positions in their companies that would be a fit for your next career opportunity.

Here are some examples:

National Social Sorority Town, State   January 2013 – Present
Vice-President of Membership   November 2014 – November 2015
  + Developed and managed action plan and budget of $10,000 for recruitment of 80 members in Spring.
  + Exceeded recruitment goals by 20% for national organization based on quota for ABC Greek system.
  + Created team activities to execute local goals and motivate retention of members.

Men's Fundraising Organization   Town, State   August 2010 – July 2013
Philanthropy Chairperson

- Designed plans for 150 members' activities raising $50,000 in funds to support local philanthropy.
- Negotiated pricing with twenty vendors for golf tournament locations, prize donations, and catering.

Business Organization   Fall 2018 – Present
Networking Committee   Old Town, New State   Spring 2018

- Developing concept, agenda, venue, content, and timeline for execution for annual dinner for 30 members.
- Schedule and organize presentations on various networking topics from guest speakers monthly.

• • •

Volunteer organizations that are locally, regionally or nationally recognized are also important to include in your resume. 'Work/Life Balance' is very important to employers – balanced employees won't 'burn out' on the job - and showing that you have integrated some volunteer experience into your life helps to show that you have found ways to create balance for yourself.

Be careful not to include every experience – just the relevant ones. Remember that the first page is the one that will be the most read (and sometimes the ONLY one), so if it doesn't warrant putting it on the first page, think about whether it should be included at all. Volunteering at an animal rescue shelter a few hours a month is a great thing, but will the hiring manager at ABC company care? Each position you apply for should dictate what 'stays' and what 'goes' from your resume.

Senior Support   Town, State   Fall 2016 – Fall 2018

- Volunteer for local shelter with 75 club members to teach crafts and arts to more than eighty seniors.

Big Siblings Organization   New Town, State   July 2010 – Present

- Selected to mentor high school student for one year, after interview process with eighteen other candidates.
- Coordinate bi-weekly activities including extracurricular events resulting in improved self-esteem for the individual.

• • •

My 'Professional Affiliations' show
my industry interest I think...

As your career progresses, joining a professional association specific to your industry or field is a great way to network and build professional relationships. Each industry or area of specialization may or may not have a local chapter in your geography, but there may be online options to attend 'e-conferences' or 'webinars'.

Whether you note these on your resume is dependent upon how actively you are involved in the organization and why you are involved. If you are a 'member on paper' – you don't attend meetings or events – then hiring managers would not necessarily need to know. In the interview process, if you were asked about your involvement in the association and the answer would be 'I really don't go to anything, but I get their newsletter', think about whether you really want to include it in the resume.

Some professional associations only have newsletters and email communication, but provide certifications and licensing to the members that are necessary or relevant to the industry. In this case the association would be very relevant. It's important to list the licensing or certification received through the organization either in bullet points under the association name or you could move this content down to the next section 'Licenses and Certifications' and not have a 'Professional Affiliations' heading.

Just as in the 'Organization or Volunteer experience' section, if you have a leadership position within a professional association, be sure to include the title, dates of the position, responsibilities, and achievements.

In this section as well as in the organization section, please do not include how many 'hours per month' you are involved. It is not important 'how much' but rather 'what did you accomplish or learn' in the experiences.

• • •

My 'Licenses and Certifications'
are relevant I think....

This section really applies people in certain fields or industries. If you are in education and have received certificates for special education areas (language, special needs etc), then you can list those certificates here. They also could go into the Education section so you choose what makes more sense – if you are applying for a job specifically in that field, we would rather see it up higher in the resume. Same situation with specialized technical certificates for engineering, architecture, CIS, etc.

Some of you may have gotten a license that may not apply to the job you are applying for – please don't include it. When someone with a real estate license is trying to get into a development or construction oriented company it may make sense to include that information because they learned something about the industry. This is definitely too much information for a resume being submitted for an administrative position outside that field. Ultimately, if the information would make a hiring manager question 'why did they include this' or 'will this take time away from the job I am hiring them for' then it should be kept off your resume.

When listing licenses include the date of expiration and on certificates the date you earned the certification. If the location of the licensure or certification is relevant, be sure to note this also.

Certifications and Specialized Training:

Level I ESL Certification	Anytown, Anywhere	March 2016
Personal Assessment Training	Anytown, Anywhere	December 2015
Henry Blanchar Communication Seminar	Anytown, Anywhere	April 2012

Professional Licensure

State Electrician License   Old Town, State   Expires May 2023

CERTIFICATIONS:

* Smartphone 2018 – LCD Training and Certification
  Anytown, Anywhere
  February 2018

* HTML Coding Specialist – HI Tech Conference
  Anytown, Anywhere
  December 2017

• • •

My 'Technical/Computer Skills'

section explains my abilities I think....

We know you can use a computer to create a resume, but what programs you can use and on what types of computers is important and every resume should have this section. There are some tenured workers who don't use a computer much, so where possible reinforce the great technical benefits you can offer an employer. Make sure to include if you can 'Mac' and 'PC' – flexibility in your computer skills is valuable.

Being able to take 'red eye' out of your family's pictures in Photoshop doesn't make it relevant to the job – unless it's a photography one- so think about that before you include it for certain employers. Graphic arts/design/architecture candidates need to list ALL relevant programs for the job. Same situation for CIS, engineering, or other technical fields. Evaluate what you include based on the job description and the company.

What if you learned how to 'manage a database' or 'use ABC internal computer system' at a job – include this in the job under work experience. Those of you who are in journalism, broadcasting, media have another whole set of programs to make sure and include. Social media networking (Facebook® and LinkedIn® and blogging etc.) could also be important to include depending on the position. The bottom line is if you would use those skills or programs at the job, include them!

Technical Skills: Mac Programs, Microsoft Visio, HTML coding, Adobe Flash

COMPUTER SKILLS   Microsoft Office Suite and Macintosh Pages, Numbers, and Notes, Blog software

Technological Skills: Microsoft Word, Excel, PowerPoint, Macintosh Pages, Dreamweaver, Adobe Illustrator

• • •

My 'Language Skills' section
accurately represents me I think ...

Not everyone will have this section on their resume. Some candidates took high school language and haven't used it since. Others may have taken a language that seemed really great at the time, but you would have to move or travel overseas to use it - that's fine and it might be included depending on the job or company you are applying for.

Whether the job specifically lists 'Spanish language skills preferred' or not, there are some languages that we recommend would be included on every resume: Spanish, Asian languages, Arabic, Italian and Portuguese (similar in structure to Spanish), American Sign Language

What if you lived in Germany for overseas study or military service, and you might be able to hold a conversation, but probably not a very long one? Probably best not to include that language, unless it would really help an employer in the workplace. Should you include your French language skills if you took it in high school and college – if it's relevant to the geography or job or industry, then put it on your resume. Same situation with Latin, Greek, and pretty much any other language we didn't already list.

Let's say your mother always spoke to you in Dutch and you under-stand it fluently and converse, read, and write it. Then you have to make the call if this would be a benefit to show your ability to be multi-cultural – we would say "yes" but be prepared. If you have a

Dutch interviewer and you can't carry on a conversation if asked to, that would be a disaster!

Language Skills   Conversationally proficient in Spanish

LANGUAGE SKILLS: Fluent in Mandarin Chinese
Conversationally fluent in Russian

• • •

My resume is ready

to go I think ....

Here's a final checklist to help you make sure you have a resume that will get a recruiter or hiring manager's attention:

- Font size no smaller than 10pt and margins no smaller than .4 all around
    - Margins should be as similar as possible on top to bottom and left to right. It looks really bad to have a 1" margin on the left and .5" on the right!

- First page has the MOST important information – they may not get to the second page!
- No excessive lines (underlining some content is ok), no bubbles – yes, we have received resumes with bubbles - no pictures of yourself (unless you are applying internationally), no graphics (unless you are in the arts or design etc.).
    - Some companies use software to 'screen out' resumes – some of that software will dump resumes with lines separating sections or across the top or down the side into the 'trash file' in their system before anyone actually could get a chance to read it.
    - A resume is not supposed to be a 'work of art' – it's a business document. Lines may have 'separated resumes from the bunch' when candidates mailed resumes to employers, but in the electronic form it won't make your resume stand out and could create a downloading problem.

- Contact information is complete and appropriate for a business document
- Clear Objective specific to the company and position OR Professional Summary with specific skills and industry information on where you mastered the skills
- Education information has all awards, degree information, and graduation date listed
- Work experience includes all relevant work including internships and externships
  - Bullet points under the jobs, NOT paragraphs
  - Reverse chronological order - most recent at the top, to least recent
  - Meaningful RESULTS in the bullet points – no Miss America bullets
  - Don't use "I" in the bullet points, or anywhere else on your resume, it's your resume so we know you did it

- Military experience is included and complete if applicable
- Organizations, volunteer, and professional affiliation experience which is detailed with accomplishments and positions held – update your social media with Connections from these organizations also
- Industry or position specific licenses or certifications are included
- Computer and special technical skills are listed – don't forget to list PC, Mac, and industry specific programs
- Language skills are listed with a definition of your level of ability

One last note:

Don't put 'References Available', 'References upon Request', or anything about references on your resume

- If we want to hire you, we will have you fill out an application and ask for references for a background check
- Putting this on your resume just takes up space you could use for information we want to know!

Now you can check out a few examples of 'Before' and 'After' resumes....

• • •

Susan Jacobson
555 N. Wilson Road
New Town, State 20000
(555) 555 - 1212

KEY OBJECTIVE
A driven individual seeking full time employment within a organization in order to utilize my skills and promote company growth.

EDUCATION
A State University   Expected Graduation: May 2010
Famous Person School of Communication
Bachelor of Science: Communication
Minor: Marketing
A Bachelor of Science in Communication with a sub-concentration in Marketing.

EXPERIENCE
Specialty Retailer – Department Manager   Jan. 04 – Present
Build solid relationships with all clients. Coordinate with different companies that help us with buying and promoting products while I communicate with our PR firm.

Healthcare Company Services – HR Assistant   Aug. 02 – Dec. 03
Build and maintain relationships with clients and employees. Organized events for all of the employees and clients to better familiarize them with the company and increase sales. Management asked me to create a new marketing campaign for customers.

Local Film Festival – Foreign Country– Intern   May 02 – June 02
This internship provided me with knowledge of the film industry. Worked directly with producers, directors, and actors. Learned about language in the entertainment industry.

Cable TV Show Pilot – Promotions Person   April 02 – May 02
Developed ideas that would help promote a reality television show. This position gave me the ability to work hand in hand with the auditioning crew of the show. Used the Visio Database system daily.

ACTIVITIES AND AWARDS
Chi Beta – A State University   Aug. 06 – Present
Chi Beta is committed to community service, support of the Greek Life organizations on A State University's campus, and national support of our philanthropies.

   Offices held:
   - Pledge President – Organized all the events, education, and chapter schedule programs for the Pledges.
   - Vice President for Membership – Created events, senior week, and house retreat that everyone attended.
   - Recruitment Person – Maintained a group of women and helped them through the process of recruitment

Susan Jacobson

555 N. Wilson Road
New Town, State 20000
(555) 555-1212
jacobson.susan@gmail.com

OBJECTIVE
To utilize my creativity, customer relationship development, and communication skills to increase efficiency as a Production Assistant in the Alphabet Networks organization.

EDUCATION
A State University   Old Town, State   May 2010
Famous Person School of Communication
Bachelor of Science in Communication   Minor: Marketing

WORK EXPERIENCE
Specialty Retailer   Old Town, State   January 2004 – Present
Department Manager
- Develop partnerships with clients such as Old Town Magazine, Blue Horse, and Adam Trellis fashions, resulting in a 30% increase in revenue.
- Coordinate media relations activities such as promotional events with advertising in five local magazines and news publications.
- Collaborate with six salespeople on quarterly sales objectives with consistent communication.

Healthcare Company Services   Old Town, State   August 2002 – December 2003
HR Assistant
- Built and maintained relationships with over 30 clients and 25 employees through consistent communication of company directives and goal attainment.
- Organized four client appreciation events for employees to network with new and existing clients.
- Created system for filing client records which increased efficiency for staff members.

Local Film Festival   Foreign City, Country   May 2002 – June 2002
Intern
- Communicated agendas and timelines with 15 producers, directors, and actors from the US.
- Created timeline and coordinated transportation for talent to travel to and from Film Festival.

Cable TV Show Pilot   Parents' Town, State   April 2002 – May 2002
Promotions Person
- Created Facebook® page for show including cast member profiles and shooting schedules.
- Surveyed community members on content, name, and creative logo for a local cable pilot.
- Assisted with pre-production details such as casting, wardrobe, set design, and prop purchases.
- Managed phone calls from agencies and locations to arrange timely shooting for scenes.

ORGANIZATIONAL EXPERIENCE
Chi Beta Sorority   Old Town, State   August 2006 – Present
Vice President of Membership Development   November 2007 – November 2008
- Developed and executed events (Senior Week and House Retreat) for 110 members including contracting with the hotel, selecting menu items, and planning the agenda.
Recruitment Counselor   August 2007 – September 2007
- Managed and supported 30 new A State students through the process of recruitment with 95% attaining membership into national sororities.

COMPUTER SKILLS
Microsoft Word, Excel, and PowerPoint, Adobe Flash, FinalCut Pro, Facebook® page development

Andrea Thompson
1234 N. Street
City, State 00000

(cell) 555-555-1212   athompson@school.org
(home) 555-555-1313   iliketofish@gmail.com

Objective   To secure a Vice-Principal opportunity in the City Independent District.

Teaching Experience

2009 - Present   Elementary School Second Grade
                    City Independent School District
                    • Primary grade teacher with experience in committees and leadership
                    • Asked to be involved with site selections and criteria
                    • Responsible for teaching students test requirements

2008 - 2009 Other Elementary School – Student Teaching Assignment
                    City Independent School District
                    • Watched mentor teacher for first grade class
                    • Supervised children during recess
                    • Learned new computer system with blackboard

Educational Background

August 2010   City University of State
                    Masters Degree in Elementary Education

May 2004   A State University
                    Bachelor of Arts in Education
                    Minor: Humanities

Other Certificates and Achievements

January 2010   Special Education Reading Certification – Primary Grades

2010   City District Teacher of the Year 2010

2009   Early Childhood Endorsement 2009

2009   ESL Certified

Member of the State Reading Council and Teacher's Association for State Standards

Asked to be a New Teacher Mentor

Worked on district team aligning reading curriculum to State Standards

References Upon Request

Andrea Thompson
1234 N. Street
City, State 00000
555-555-1212
athompson@school.org

Objective: To utilize curriculum and program development, communication, organization, and student development skills as a Vice-Principal for City Independent District.

Teaching Experience:

Elementary School Second Grade City, State Fall 2009 - Present
City Independent District
Second Grade Teacher

- Improved standardized test scores for three 'rotating' classes by 15% in 2010 versus 2009.
- Communicate with 5 teachers in weekly meetings to maximize productivity in instruction and discuss progress of students in each classroom environment.
- Chosen by Principal to act as Site Coordinator for social studies program in 2010–2011 school year.
- Identified new technology for primary grades to increase focus and retention of information which was implemented in all District schools by year-end 2010.
- Instruct American history curriculum to 30 students using Blackboard, visual aids, district text, group projects, and various testing methods.

Other Elementary School City, State Fall 2008 – Spring 2009
City Independent District
Student Teacher

- Collaborated with Mentor Teacher to instruct history curriculum to 25 first grade students.
- Monitored safety of over 80 children during recess time and organized game activities on elementary school playground.
- Learned Blackboard computer system for teaching which increased test scores from students by more than 20% during the semester.

Certifications and Specialized Educational Training
Special Education Reading Certification – Primary Grades State January 2010
Early Childhood Endorsement State August 2010
ESL Certified State May 2009

Professional Awards and Recognition
City Independent District Interview Team State 2009 - Present
- Selection Committee Member for 3 Principals, 1 Vice Principal, and 15 Teachers into school district.

City District Teacher of the Year State 2010
- Nominated by parents and administrators in recognition of outstanding teaching performance.

City Independent District New Teacher Mentor State 2009 - 2010

Professional Associations
Teachers' Association for State Standards City, State January 2010 - Present

State Reading Council City, State August 2009 – Present

Educational Background
City University of State City, State August 2010
Masters of Arts in Elementary Education

A State University City, State May 2004
Bachelor of Arts in Education
Minor: Humanities

Jacqueline Happerstadt
800 W. Street - City, State 00000
Jhappers724@hotmail.com – 555-555-1212

Summary:
Results oriented professional with substantial achievement and demonstrated success in highly competitive and constantly changing technical companies.

Professional Experience:
ABC Technical Company

Project Coordinator/Account Person
(Aug 2005 – Present)

Helped large projects run smoothly by talking with internal teams such as Distribution Center, Customer Service Center, and Billing
Managed and coordinated multiple projects for XYZ Large Client Corp.
Developed project management skills by working with AQ Organization
Led modification and upgrade of internal software system making it more user-friendly and efficient
Met Federal requirements to mail controlled substances
Initiated relationships and gained customer loyalty with clients while helping to solve problems find solutions and satisfy needs
Contributed tremendously to project profitability while developing innate leadership abilities

XYZ Technical Company

Financial Analyst, Supply Chain Department
(July 2003 - July 2005)

Controlled overhead expense budget for Supply Chain Organization
Planned and forecasted budgets for many departments
Worked with high level managers on actions plans and targets for the G&A budget
Coordinated resources for customers in US, Canada, Mexico, and Latin America
Willing to take on varied projects not in current job scope
Improved time management skills because of strict deadlines

Non-International Finance Lead, Supply Chain Department
(Jan 2003 -June 2003)

Performed as the Team lead for disbursements and freight processes
Heightened public relations skills in developing relationships with delivery providers
Developed managerial skills managing and leading several contractors
Led department for creation of controlled and ready – to - audit processes

Print Division, Sales Internship
(June 2002-Dec 2002)

Tracked and measured information for sales representatives
Shadowed a Print Sales Representative for 1 week
Strengthened sales skills by taking the XYZ Special Technique Sales courses
Created and implemented methods to collect and analyze sales goals
Participated in internal audits for the Client Relations Management process

Education:
Bachelor of Science in Business Administration - GPA: 3.5
Dual Major: Finance and Marketing (Graduation: Dec 2002)
University of State, Town, State

Organization:
Beta Omega Chi Sorority Alumnae Association Secretary (Aug 2008 – Aug 08)
College Chapter Secretary (Nov 2000 – Nov 2001)

Computer Skills: Excel, Power Point, Hyperion Qbase, TRIO, Warehouse Balance Systems

Jacqueline Happerstadt

800 W. Street   City, State 00000
(555) 555-1212
Jhapperstadt1@aol.com

Objective: To secure a Financial Sales Specialist position in a dynamic sales organization to utilize business skills including results achievement, verbal and written communication, project development and account management.

Professional Experience:

ABC Technical Company

Project Coordinator/Account Person   City, State   August 2005 – Present
- Contributed to project profitability with responsibility for 80% of annual company revenue.
- Coordinate with six internal department teams such as Distribution Center, Customer Service Center, and Billing to meet customer objectives and deadlines.
- Manage and coordinate more than twelve ongoing annual financial planning and product development projects for XYZ Large Corporation.
- Developed project management process for AQ Organization resulting in $250,000 reduced costs.
- Led team on six month upgrade of internal software systems for increased department efficiency.
- Complied with Federal requirements to ship controlled substances to more than 10,000 customers.
- Analyzed customer problems and created solutions to satisfy client needs monthly.

XYZ Technical Company

Financial Analyst, Supply Chain Department   City, State   July 2003 - July 2005
- Managed $40 million overhead expense budget for Supply Chain organization.
- Planned and forecasted quarterly and annual budgets for operating expense and freight.
- Collaborated with senior level management in multiple departments to develop quarterly action plans, targets and analysis for the G&A budget.
- Coordinated resources for 10,000 customers in US, Canada, Mexico, and Latin America.
- Met state and federal deadlines through consistent email communication with 120 internal and external team members.

Non-International Finance Lead, Supply Chain Department   January 2003 - June 2003
- Team lead over twenty people for the domestic disbursements freight payment process.
- Developed relationships with forty transportation providers through customer service programming.
- Managed and led seven contractors resulting in four internal promotions and 100% goal attainment.
- Created controlled, audit-ready processes which improved efficiency and department morale.

Printing Systems Division, Sales Internship   June 2002 - December 2002
- Tracked and measured monthly financial data for 1400 sales representatives.
- Shadowed a Print Sales Representative on sales calls to learn XYZ sales methods.
- Successfully completed sales skills training through the XYZ Special Technique Sales courses.
- Created computer based methodology to collect and analyze sales versus goal attainment.
- Assisted with three internal audits for the Client Relations Management processes.

Organization Experience:

Beta Omega Chi National Panhellenic Sorority   Town, State   September 1998 - Present
Alumnae Association Secretary   August 2007 – August 2008
- Responsible for accurate record maintenance on meetings and member information for chapter.
- Coordinate monthly meetings for over fifty alumnae to participate in community based activities.
Collegiate Chapter Secretary   November 2000 – November 2001
- Managed confidential information, records, and national reports for chapter of 150 members.

Education:

University of State   Town, State   December 2002
Bachelor of Science in Business Administration
Major: Finance and Marketing

Computer Skills: Microsoft Excel, Microsoft Power Point, Microsoft Word, Hyperion Qbase, TRIO

Jonathan Allen Anderson
123 N. Central Street
New Town, State 99999
(555) 555-1212
Jall2491max@gmail.com

Executive Objective:

I would like to secure a challenging career opportunity to share my academic, organization, and technology skills.

Educational Work:
September 2008–
May 2012

New State University – New Town, State
Bachelor of Arts with a concentration in Business and Communication   GPA: 3.13

Professional Work:
March 2006 –
Present

Anderson Medical Supplies – New Town, State
Project Coordinator

Work with people to create calendar events
Assist with project around marketing and sales goals
Help salespeople learn different key types of technology
I learned ways to work with computer programs and databases while I provided certification to team members internally.
Follow procedures for arranging meetings and conferences off-site
Contract with bid teams for new and old vendors to use on different projects
Responsible for having people report details of their part of the events to the managers

December 1999 –
January 2006

Main College– New Town, State
Student Assistant

Grade papers for professor and help to teach lessons
Give presentations with power points and videos
Responsible for assisting professor with paperwork including inputting grades
Answer phones and questions when people call the office

Military Work
May 1996 –
November 1999

US Armed Forces Branch – Internationally based in multiple locations
Sergeant Level 1
Finished missions as requested by senior officers
Worked on technical projects and honorably discharged

Volunteer Work
January 2005 –
June 2005

Special Interest Group Foundation – New Town, State
Asked people to donate for sponsorships and tickets at annual event.

Professional Groups

Education Association – New Town, State
Treasurer and Member– May 2000 – October 2005
Ensure funds are available to support costs for speakers and events
Help fellow educators to realize their career dreams

Accomplishments

Received 'Employee of Quarter' at Anderson Medical Supplies 2006
Chosen to 'on-board' new employees consistently
Selected to present at New Student Orientation 2004
Honorable Discharge 1999

Technical Skills

Microsoft, Mac, Level 3 Armed Forces Database Program, Adobe Photoshop

Other Skills

Excellent communication skills
Able to work in teams or individually
Speak Latin and Spanish
Identified as a leader in multiple positions and projects

Professional References are available upon request

John Anderson

123 N. Central Street
Anytown, State 99999
(555) 555-1212
janderson@gmail.com

Executive Objective:

To secure a career opportunity with ABC Company as a XYZ Manager which will use my leadership, organization, and technology skills to increase revenue and profitability.

Professional Work:

March 2004 – **Anderson Medical Supplies**   New Town, State
Present   Project Coordinator
- Received 'Employee of Quarter' award for exceptional meeting programs in Q3 2006.
- Chosen to mentor five new employees for internal database training and on-boarding.
- Create weekly department specific calendar events through Outlook Express resulting in 25% increase in accuracy and employee participation.
- Assist with marketing and sales projects to provide reports and information for quarterly analysis and planning.
- Train salespeople on Microsoft and Mac programs for internal and external reporting monthly.
- Certify sales team members on appropriate use of internal programs with 100% compliance.
- Arrange weekly meetings and regional conferences off-site including location, agenda, and contract content evaluation and approval.
- Contract with eight internal bid teams to determine new and old vendors for annual projects.

December 1999- **Main College**   New Town, State
January 2006   Student Assistant
- Selected to present student organization information at New Student Orientation event in 2004.
- Organized grading system for papers which improved professor's efficiency in reporting.
- Presented class content weekly by effectively using Power Point and videos where possible.
- Communicated class information to students and faculty through phone and email as needed.

Military Work:

May 1996 –   **US Armed Forces Branch**   Internationally based in multiple locations
November 1999 Sergeant Level 1
- Awarded Honorable Discharge in November 1999.
- Developed and executed Security program with a training plan and documentation on consequences of violation for the crews.
- Created monthly plan for distribution of XYZ security patches, software upgrades, and system configuration changes resulting in reduced downtime for daily operations.
- Completed over fifteen missions across three countries as assigned by senior officers.

Volunteer Work:

January 2005 – **Special Interest Group Foundation**   New Town, State
June 2005   Volunteer
- Coordinated $2500 in donations including four sponsorships and ticket sales at annual event.
- Collaborated with team of fifty volunteers to execute charity event raising $200,000 annually.

Professional Groups:

May 2000 -   **Education Association**   New Town, State
October 2005   Treasurer and Member
- Managed $25K budget to support costs for monthly speakers and quarterly member events.
- Mentored sixteen new members on organization structure and networking opportunities.

Technical Skills: Microsoft OS, Mac Programs, Level 3 Armed Forces Database Program

Language Skills: Proficient in reading, writing, and speaking Spanish

Educational Work:

May 2005   **New State University**   New Town, State
               Bachelor of Arts – Business   GPA: 3.1
               Dean's List 2003, Spring 2005

Ashia Stevens-Campbell

39000 N. Patrick Circle, Town, State 05000   602-555-1212   acampbell09432@yahoo.com

Highly motivated, energetic and hard-working individual looking for a challenging opportunity.

SUMMARY OF QUALIFICATIONS

- Experienced in program execution and client services
- Strong work ethic and high level of professionalism
- Excellent oral and written communication skills
- Bilingual English/Spanish

WORK HISTORY

Mountain Mental Health Center
HBT Program --Lead Therapist   April 2003-Present
- Primary therapist for at-risk youth participants
- Supervise behavioral health technicians
- Coordinate Child-Family Team meetings
- Communicate with school faculty and juvenile probation
- On-going contact with parents and guardians of participants

HomeCare, Inc. /State Job Corps.
Career Development Counselor   October 2002-April 2003
- Serve as a guide for youth ages 16-24, throughout their entire Job Corps. Program; managing a caseload of 25 or more youth in the Security vocation
- Coordinate staffing for trainees who require further accommodations

County Correctional Services
Counselor IV   November 2000-October 2002
- Serve as advocate for seriously mentally ill patients incarcerated in county jail
- Engage patients in group discussions
- Oversee basic care of patients, including psychiatric and medical
- Communicate with correctional officers, psychiatrists, and other medical staff
- Coordinate staffing with Value Options case managers to address patient's transition into the community

Lakeside Social Services
Contract Counselor   July 1998-October 2000
- Serve as primary counselor for all ages and facilitate individual, group, and family sessions
- Communicate with other counselors and administrative staff
- Manage a caseload of 10 or more clients
- Attend weekly staffing meetings with psychological consultant

EDUCATION

State School of Real Estate and Business (2003), Licensed Real Estate Agent   License #411

Master of Science Mental Health Counseling (2000), University of Saint Peter
Bachelor of Arts Psychology (1998), Pristine University

Ashia Stevens-Campbell

39000 N. Patrick Circle
Town, State 05000
acampbell@earthlink.net 602-555-1212

Professional Summary: Business professional with experience in public healthcare and management including client evaluation, personnel management, communication, and program development and execution.

Work Experience:

Mountain Mental Health Center

HBT Program - Lead Therapist   Town, State   April 2003 - Present
- Primary therapist for up to 100 at-risk youth participants with fluency in Spanish and interaction with parents and students.
- Coordinate Child-Family Team meetings for successful resolution of issues in 100% of incidents.
- Communicate ongoing with school faculty and juvenile probation in written and verbal formats including group family environments.

HomeCare, Inc. /State Job Corps.

Career Development Counselor   Town, State   October 2002 - April 2003
- Managed a caseload of more than twenty-five youth in the Security vocation.
- Coordinated staffing for trainees who required further accommodations with successful placement in over 90% of all cases.
- Trained four new counselors on policies and procedures related to intake processing and programs.

County Correctional Health Services

Counselor IV   Town, State   November 2000 – October 2002
- Served as advocate to state facilities for seriously mentally ill patients incarcerated in county jail.
- Communicated with more than fifty correctional officers, psychiatrists, and other medical staff via email and in written reports about patient progress.
- Coordinated staffing with Options case managers to address patient's transition into the community and workforce through funded programming.

Lakeside Social Services

Contract Counselor   Town, State   July 1998 - October 2000
- Designated as primary counselor for facilitation of individual, group, and family sessions weekly.
- Collaborated with ten other counselors and five administrative staff for increased efficiency in processing up to twenty patients quarterly.
- Managed personal caseload of 10 or more clients from entrance in programs to discharge into external resources locally.
- Attended weekly staffing meetings with psychological consultant to review patients' progress.

Education:

University of Saint Peter   Town, State
Master of Science in Mental Health Counseling   May 2000

Pristine University   Town, State   May 1998
Bachelor of Arts in Psychology

Language Skills: Fluent in Spanish

Computer Skills: Microsoft Word and Microsoft Excel

Michael Adamstone

555 W. Main Street
New Town, State 90000
(555) 555-1212
Madamstone5183@gmail.com

OBJECTIVE

To obtain employment with a retail store

TRAITS/ SKILLS

- Positive team player
- Excellent verbal and written communication
- Hard-working and motivated individual

EDUCATION
8/03- 5/07

University of State   New Town, State
G.P.A. 3.83; Magna cum Laude
Major: History
Minor: Portuguese
Portugal Exchange University   Foreign Town, Portugal

Computer skills with Microsoft Office, Macintosh, and Dreamweaver programs

WORK EXPERIENCE
Fall 2007 - Present

Mark's Shoe Store   New Town, State
Salesperson
- Highest sales in the department every month since starting
- Interacted with customers to assess their needs in footwear
- Used product knowledge to effectively sell products customers liked

Summer 2006

New Expensive Store at the Mall   New Town, State
Salesperson in the Really Expensive Shirts department
- Applied skills in customer service
- Trained to use register

Summer 03, 04, 05

Carson's Medical Equipment Inc.   New Town, State
Billing Assistant
- Developed understanding of how to respond to the requests of management
- Learned time management skills

Summer 2002

Point of No Return Sports Center   New Town, State
Desk Person
- Used and further developed communication skills in working with clients
- Learned to be responsible and reliable in managing monthly dues of clients

ORGANIZATIONS
8/04 - Present
8/05 - 05/07
12/06 – 05/07
3/06 - 05/07

Gamma Alpha Theta
Lambda Pi Alpha Historical Honor Society
Sigma Lambda Omega National Leadership and Honors Organization
Phi Beta Kappa Honor Society

AWARDS AND HONORS
Spring/Fall 05/Spring 06
Spring 07

Dean's List Honorable Mention
Dean's List

REFERENCES

Available upon request

Michael Adamstone
555 W. Main Street
New Town, State 90000
(555) 555-1212   madamstone@gmail.com

OBJECTIVE

To obtain a sales position utilizing my communication, interpersonal, and organization skills within a specialty retail store to generate increased profit.

WORK EXPERIENCE

September 2007 – Present | **Mark's Shoe Store** | New Town, State
Salesperson
• Awarded 'Highest Sales' monthly from September 2007.
• Develop relationships with more than 200 clients monthly.
• Consulted with management on new concepts for merchandising and sales which led to 20% increase in sales monthly.
• Assist with inventory management reducing returns and damages 30%.
• Create window displays weekly to promote sale items and increasing retail sales for a store with over $500,000 annual revenue.

June 2006 – August 2006 | **New Expensive Store at the Mall** | New Town, State
Salesperson
• Chosen for Really Expensive Shirt section helping over 50 clients weekly.
• Trained on Sales and Customer Service processes over a two week period.
• Accurately managed monetary transactions with 100% balances at shift end.

Summers
2003, 2004, 2005 | **Carson's Medical Equipment Inc.** | New Town, State
Billing Assistant
• Organized confidential client information including billing through forty managed care companies such as Medicare.
• Constructed sales training materials with information from ten vendors.
• Completed office reorganization including filing and phone system change.

May 2002 – August 2002 | **Point of No Return Sports Center** | New Town, State
Desk Assistant
• Communicated with 250 clients weekly on membership and game questions.
• Managed monthly dues of clients securing 90% on time payment.

ORGANIZATION and VOLUNTEER EXPERIENCE

January 2008 – Present | **American Volunteer Association** | New Town, State
Member Coordinator
• Plan membership recruitment events at local venues for networking.

August 2004 – Present | **Gamma Alpha Theta National Fraternity** | New Town, State

EDUCATION

May 2007 | **University of State** | New Town, State
Major: History
Minor: Portuguese | Magna cum Laude Honors (3.8 GPA)
Dean's List Spring and Fall 2005, Spring 2006, Spring 2007

May 2006 - August 2006 | **Portugal Exchange University** | Foreign Town, Portugal
• Collaborated with international students on presentations and research.
• Gained knowledge and sensitivity of cross-cultural lifestyle practices.

December 2006 – May 2007 | **Sigma Alpha Lambda National Leadership and Honors Organization**

March 2006 – May 2007 | **Phi Beta Kappa Honor Society**

TECHNOLOGICAL SKILLS   Microsoft Office Suite, Macintosh Pages and Notes, Dreamweaver

I think

Elizabeth Colter

555 E. Broadway Rd
New Town, State 80000

(555) 555 - 1212
Lizc48239@
hotmail.com

Objective

To obtain an administrative role within a large company

Employment History

Assistant Office Manager

Fall 2006 – Summer 2008 ABC High School, New Town, State

- Work with secretarial staff on making copies, answering phones, and questions
- Talk to parents and children when they come in needing help
- Meet requests of principal and teachers as asked
- Make sure all staff have information on school materials
- Order office supplies when we need them

Assistant Office Secretary

Fall 2003 – Fall 2006 ABC High School, New Town, State

- Aided in daily communication with parents and students
- Copied tests and other materials for all teachers
- Met with staff and principal on issues about office operations

Secretarial and Financial Assistant

Winter 2001 – Fall 2003 Family Owned Company, New Town, State

- Assisted in daily secretarial needs, such as word processing and customer service
- Worked on payroll, billing, and bidding processes

Tutor for struggling and troubled children

Fall 2001 – Summer 2003 New Town, State

- Worked with hard-to-handle third and fourth graders
- Taught and strengthened their skills to read and write
- Helped them reach the level of their classmates

Other Experience

Current member of State Administrative Association

Speak and understand Mandarin Chinese very well

Mac and PC user at work

Education

Fall 1998	ABC High School, New Town, State	GPA 3.00
Spring 2007	A State College – Associates of Arts in Business	GPA 3.52

Elizabeth Colter
555 E. Broadway Road
New Town, State 80000
(555) 555-1212
<u>elizabeth.colter@state.edu</u>

Objective: To utilize my communication, interpersonal, and organizational skills to secure an administrative position with a dynamic real estate development organization.

Work Experience:

ABC High School   New Town, State   September 2006 – May 2008
Assistant Office Manager
- Collaborate with team of five office staff on daily office management for 50 teachers and principal.
- Organize office duties into weekly rotation allowing maximization of staff development annually.
- Meet with parents and students as needed to resolve communication or school operation issues.
- Distribute weekly and monthly newsletter to staff regarding processes for ordering supplies.
- Manage inventory for all school materials related to copies, textbooks, machines, and office supplies.

Assistant Office Secretary   October 2003 – September 2006
- Coordinated administrative tasks including filing and phone reception at school with 450 students.
- Interacted with 80 teachers, students, and office staff at weekly meetings and for individual needs.
- Maintained test and curriculum materials for teachers to have organized filing systems.

Family Owned Company   New Town, State   December 2001 – October 2003
Office and Financial Assistant
- Processed payroll, account billing, and customer bids which increased profitability by 25% annually.
- Managed confidential financial transactions and client database for 15 employees monthly.
- Created positive environment for over fifty new and existing customers through elevated customer service and attention to detail.

Teaching Assistance   New Town, State   October 2001 – June 2003
Tutor
- Created worksheets and tests for primary grade students on a weekly basis.
- Motivated exceptional academic performance through 'check-in' competitions with peers.
- Communicated student progress to parents through weekly email reports.

Organizational Experience:

State Administrative Association   New Town, State   August 2006 - Present
Personal Development Chair   November 2007 - Present
- Organize monthly speakers for chapter meetings on topics including networking and professionalism while managing a budget of $4,000.
- Coordinate monthly calendar for events with eighteen organizations in the business community.

Educational Experience:

A State College   New Town, State   Spring 2007
Associate of Arts in Business   GPA: 3.5

Language Skills: Conversationally proficient in Mandarin Chinese

Computer Skills: Microsoft Word, Microsoft Excel and Microsoft Power Point
                      Macintosh Pages, Macintosh Numbers, and Macintosh Notes

I think™

49

PAMELA HENRY

14000 S. First Place • City, State 00000
(555) 555-1212 – home • (555) 555-1213 – cell • pmhenry@net.net

Summary: Experienced, driven management and marketing person recognized for strong leadership capabilities, dedication and determination with solid communication skills and abilities to build quality relationships and create new partnership programs.

Experience

State Sports Company (a.k.a. Sports Events America)   **Town, State**
Marketing Assistant Manager   01/2006-03/2008
- Developed and maintain strong, dynamic relationships with fundraising volunteer committee to ensure maximum impact for sponsorship relationships while simultaneously pursuing and developing prospective sponsors.
- Worked in conjunction with sales team, Directors Board and committees to execute branding and sales strategies, while maintaining budget quotas and negotiating profitable partnership agreements.
- Preserved relationships with community leaders and partnerships within local and national businesses.
- Managed marketing assistants for department education and research on culture and market trends.
- Implemented the first comprehensive approach to sponsorship development and sales strategies.
- Established an individual account list six months which included several community corporate headquarters.
- Fiscally supervised the accuracy of contracts relating to hospitality and promotional packages.

Assistant to Executive Manager   10/2000-01/2006
- Liaison between Marketing Department, Services Department personnel and Executive Manager.
- Responsible for all correspondence, travel and meeting schedules for Executive Manager.
- Responsible for adherence to all areas of sponsorship contracts.
- Served as main liaison to XYZ Sponsor for daily planning and execution of sponsor goals and objectives.
- Interfaced with high-level executives in all sales, service and hospitality areas.
- Managed and serviced key accounts of all levels (e.g. Anderson Corp, Professional Licensing Company).
- Cataloged all trade accounts and disseminated inventory through several departments.
- Responsible for implementation of all fiscal operations of Sales Department. Reported bi-monthly to Executive Manager on budget update.
- Executed hospitality program including travel plans and local sports teams' suites. Conceptualized and launched partner VIP program for all levels of sponsoring, culminating in the distribution of hospitality perks.

Entertainment Company ABC   **Town, State**
Assistant Ticket Manager   07/1997-05/1999
- Managed Ticket Representatives on operations of ticket office, including customer service, maintenance of accounts during busy national sports and entertainment seasons.
- Responsible for daily deposits, audits and tracking receivables from department.
- Created account relations program for sports season ticket holders and entertainment venues.

Very Large Hotel Chain   **Town, State**
Assistant Manager   08/1994-07/1997
- Directed and managed on-duty staff and provided supervision for high end resort.
- Coordinated and monitored all activities of resort employees, including hiring and development of new and existing staff members, management and supervision of department managers.
- Coordinated department activities, guest servicing and relations.
- Provided liaison between Executive Management and resort guests.

Community Service

City of State Special Works Group   **Town, State**
Committee Director   09/2007-Present
- Work with team of members to generate programs for community organization.
- Create ideas for increasing memberships with different events and ways to meet new people.

Education

State University   08/1992- 05/1994
Bachelor of Arts Degree in Tourism

Community College of State   08/1990- 05/1992
Major: Business

PAMELA HENRY

14000 S. First Place   City, State 00000
(555) 555-1213   pmhenry@net.net
www.socialmediasite.com/phenry

OBJECTIVE: To maximize profitability and efficiency for a consumer products company through effective personnel management, communication skills, and development of innovative and creative partnership opportunities.

PERSONNEL MANAGEMENT EXPERIENCE:

State Sports Company (Sports Events America) Town, State

Marketing Assistant Manager   January 2006 – March 2008
- Managed four marketing assistants for continuous department education and research on culture and market trends, including use of social media outlets, to maintain competitive focus for sponsors.
- Supervised the accuracy of all contract fulfillments related to hospitality and promotional packages.
- Motivated volunteer committee of 200 members during event activities including XYZ Big Sports Event and Special Person College Program, and ancillary programs integral to revenue generation for SSC.
- Controlled budget quotas of $3.1 million and negotiated profitable partnership agreements in excess of $850,000.

Entertainment Company ABC   Town, State

Assistant Ticket Manager   July 1997 - May 1999
- Managed twelve Ticket Representatives on operations of ticket office, including maintenance of accounts during busy national sports and entertainment seasons.
- Handle and balance daily deposits up to $50,000, and conduct audits and receivables tracking monthly.
- Created account relations program for 1000 season ticket holders, eliminating customer complaints and conflicts.

Very Large Hotel Chain   Town, State

Assistant Manager   August 1994 – July 1997
- Hired, trained, and developed thirty new staff members, while managing and supervising eight department managers to meet established departmental goals.
- Directed and managed on-duty staff and provided supervision for 4-star, 370 room, luxury resort.
- Coordinated guest services activities for a team of 500 resort employees maximizing customer service.
- Provided communication as a liaison between Executive Office and resort guests through internal weekly reports.

PROJECT MANAGEMENT EXPERIENCE

State Sports Company   Town, State

Marketing Assistant Manager   January 2006 - March 2008
- Implemented the company's first comprehensive approach to sponsorship development and sales strategies generating $6.8M in incremental revenue.
- Established an individual account portfolio generating over $450,000 in new revenue resulting in sponsorship sales with clients including Large Sports Product Company, Big Tech Corp, which exceeded 40% of annual goal.
- Maintained relationships with community leaders and partnerships within local and national businesses for 90% year to year retention of sponsorships.

Assistant to Executive Manager   October 2000 - January 2006
- Executed hospitality program including travel plans for up to 350 people and scheduling for local sports teams' suites.
- Developed and launched partner VIP program for all levels of sponsorship, involving distribution of hospitality perks such as sporting and entertainment event tickets.
- Managed and serviced 10 key accounts of all sponsor levels (e.g. Anderson Corp, Professional Licensing Company).
- Served as primary contact to XYZ Sponsor for daily planning and execution of sponsor goals and objectives.
- Cataloged all trade accounts and disseminated inventory through Logo Clothing and Logo Trinkets departments.
- Implemented all fiscal operations of Sales Department for 100% balance of inventory transactions annually.
- Reported bi-monthly to Executive Manager on budget update via Excel and Word documents.

COMMUNITY SERVICE EXPERIENCE

City of State Special Works Group   Town, State

Committee Director   September 2007 - Present
- Collaborate with 55 members generating quarterly programs for fundraising and community volunteerism.
- Create ideas for monthly events with networking opportunities to increase membership by more than 20% annually.

EDUCATION

State University   May 1994
Bachelor of Arts Degree in Tourism

COMPUTER SKILLS   Microsoft Programs, TicketPro database, Twitter

I think

51

EXTRA RESOURCES:

www.bestresumebuilder.com

- ◆ If you want to use a program which will walk you through, step by step in less than 45 minutes, the input which creates a great resume - check out this resource. Created specifically to be detailed on input to create a dynamic resume, it's specific and easy to use.

Other resume books

- ◆ If your specialty has different special circumstances, you can look for resume books tailored to your specialty. Just be careful not to over-complicate your resume for the reader!

• • •

INDEX

	Page
Address	3
Bullet points	14-17, 22
Certifications	27-28
Checklist	33-35
Chronological format	1-2
Clubs	21-23
Computer skills	29-30
Contact information	3-5
Education	9-11
Email address	4
Functional format	1-2
GPA	10
Greek Life	22
High school information	10
Internships	13
Job experience	13-15
Language skills	31-32
Licenses	27-28
Majors	9
Military Experience	19-20
Minors	9
Name	3
Objective	7-8
Organization experience	21-24
Overseas Study	12
Phone number	3-4
Professional associations	25-26
Professional Summary	7-8
References	31
Sample resumes	36-51
School information	9-12
Skills	13-14
SMART	13-14
Social media	4, 29-30, 34
Technological skills	29-30
Traits	7
Volunteer experience	24
Work experience	13-17

Also available NOW in the **I think** *Career Skills Series:*

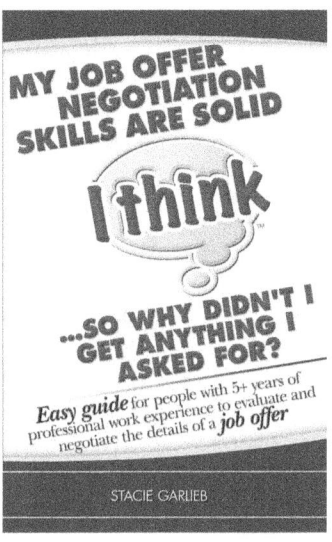

ACKNOWLEDGEMENTS

To the people I have had the privilege of working with over the past two decades that trusted me to help them represent their skills in resumes throughout their careers, thank you for helping me figure out what makes an impactful resume.

. . .

ABOUT THE AUTHOR

Stacie Garlieb is the President of Successful Impressions LLC which assists working professionals with career search processes and skills.

She has been featured several times on NBC television and radio during morning and evening news with interview tips. Stacie is a well-known national speaker who has presented on various career skills topics at events such as 'Build Your Career Event' (Career Builder/University of Phoenix), Arizona Women's Expo, American Marketing Association International Conferences Jobs for AZ Graduates Career Development Conferences, Reinvent Your Future, and multiple corporate team development sessions. Her career search tips and interview skills advice have been published in collegiate, national sorority, and alumni publications.

Stacie was invited by California State Sacramento and University of the Pacific to act as a Career Consultant to the career services departments. She developed the Career Fair Training Program for University of the Pacific, and assisted in writing the "Career Services Interview Skills" guide. Over more than twenty years, she has worked for Fortune 500 organizations in sales, marketing, and management positions with recruiting responsibility after earning her Bachelor of Science from Arizona State University.

If you would like to know more about Stacie Garlieb's company or her seminars please visit her website at www.successfulimpressions.net

• • •